50 Grandma Dessert Recipes for Home

By: Kelly Johnson

Table of Contents

- Grandma's Apple Pie
- Old-Fashioned Chocolate Cake
- Classic Lemon Bars
- Homemade Peach Cobbler
- Grandma's Blueberry Muffins
- Peanut Butter Cookies
- Butterscotch Pudding
- Coconut Cream Pie
- Oatmeal Raisin Cookies
- Banana Bread
- Blackberry Crisp
- Carrot Cake with Cream Cheese Frosting
- Snickerdoodle Cookies
- Pineapple Upside-Down Cake
- Grandma's Fudge Brownies
- Strawberry Rhubarb Pie
- Classic Rice Pudding
- Molasses Cookies
- Raspberry Thumbprint Cookies
- Chocolate Chip Banana Bread
- Old-Fashioned Bread Pudding
- Grandma's Pound Cake
- Buttermilk Biscuits with Strawberry Jam
- Peach Pie
- Lemon Meringue Pie
- Cinnamon Rolls
- Homemade Strawberry Shortcake
- Grandma's Chocolate Chip Cookies
- Blueberry Buckle
- Cherry Crisp
- Apple Crumble
- Date Squares
- Shortbread Cookies
- Coconut Macaroons
- Grandma's Gingerbread Cake

- Pecan Pie Bars
- Buttermilk Pancakes with Maple Syrup
- Chocolate Eclair Cake
- Peanut Butter Fudge
- Grandma's Snickerdoodle Bars
- Black Forest Cake
- Lemon Poppy Seed Cake
- Classic Tiramisu
- Chocolate Covered Strawberries
- Grandma's Bread and Butter Pudding
- Old-Fashioned Sugar Cookies
- Peach Melba
- Chocolate Cream Pie
- Grandma's Pumpkin Bread
- Classic Cheesecake

Grandma's Apple Pie

Ingredients:

- 2 ½ cups all-purpose flour
- 1 cup unsalted butter, cold and cubed
- 1 teaspoon salt
- 1 teaspoon granulated sugar
- 6-8 tablespoons ice water
- 6-8 medium-sized apples (such as Granny Smith), peeled, cored, and sliced
- ¾ cup granulated sugar
- ¼ cup packed brown sugar
- 1 tablespoon lemon juice
- 1 teaspoon ground cinnamon
- ¼ teaspoon ground nutmeg
- 2 tablespoons cornstarch
- 1 tablespoon unsalted butter, for dotting
- 1 egg, beaten (for egg wash)
- Additional granulated sugar (for sprinkling)

Instructions:

1. In a large mixing bowl, combine the flour, salt, and sugar. Cut in the cold cubed butter using a pastry cutter or fork until the mixture resembles coarse crumbs.
2. Gradually add ice water, 1 tablespoon at a time, tossing with a fork until the dough comes together. Divide the dough in half, shape each half into a disk, wrap them in plastic wrap, and refrigerate for at least 1 hour.
3. Preheat your oven to 400°F (200°C). On a lightly floured surface, roll out one disk of dough into a circle about ⅛ inch thick. Carefully transfer it to a 9-inch pie dish, gently pressing it into the bottom and sides.
4. In a large bowl, toss together the sliced apples, granulated sugar, brown sugar, lemon juice, cinnamon, nutmeg, and cornstarch until well combined.
5. Pour the apple mixture into the prepared pie crust, spreading it out evenly. Dot the top with small pieces of butter.
6. Roll out the second disk of dough into a circle about ⅛ inch thick. Place it over the filling. Trim any excess dough hanging over the edges and crimp the edges to seal. Cut slits in the top crust to allow steam to escape.

7. Brush the top crust with the beaten egg and sprinkle with additional granulated sugar.
8. Place the pie on a baking sheet to catch any drips and bake in the preheated oven for 45-55 minutes, or until the crust is golden brown and the filling is bubbly.
9. Allow the pie to cool on a wire rack for at least 2 hours before serving to allow the filling to set. Serve warm or at room temperature, optionally with a scoop of vanilla ice cream on top. Enjoy your Grandma's Apple Pie!

Old-Fashioned Chocolate Cake

Ingredients:

For the cake:

- 2 cups all-purpose flour
- 1 ¾ cups granulated sugar
- ¾ cup unsweetened cocoa powder
- 1 ½ teaspoons baking powder
- 1 ½ teaspoons baking soda
- 1 teaspoon salt
- 2 large eggs, at room temperature
- 1 cup whole milk
- ½ cup vegetable oil
- 2 teaspoons pure vanilla extract
- 1 cup boiling water

For the frosting:

- 1 cup unsalted butter, softened
- 3 ½ cups powdered sugar, sifted
- ½ cup unsweetened cocoa powder
- ½ teaspoon salt
- 2 teaspoons pure vanilla extract
- 4-6 tablespoons whole milk or heavy cream

Instructions:

1. Preheat your oven to 350°F (175°C). Grease and flour two 9-inch round cake pans.
2. In a large mixing bowl, sift together the flour, sugar, cocoa powder, baking powder, baking soda, and salt.
3. Add the eggs, milk, vegetable oil, and vanilla extract to the dry ingredients. Beat on medium speed with an electric mixer for 2 minutes.
4. Stir in the boiling water until the batter is well combined. The batter will be thin.
5. Pour the batter evenly into the prepared cake pans.
6. Bake in the preheated oven for 30-35 minutes, or until a toothpick inserted into the center comes out clean.
7. Remove the cakes from the oven and allow them to cool in the pans for 10 minutes. Then, transfer them to a wire rack to cool completely.

8. While the cakes are cooling, prepare the frosting. In a large mixing bowl, beat the softened butter until creamy.
9. Gradually add the sifted powdered sugar, cocoa powder, salt, and vanilla extract, mixing on low speed until combined.
10. Add the milk or cream, one tablespoon at a time, until the frosting reaches your desired consistency. Beat on medium-high speed for 2-3 minutes until light and fluffy.
11. Once the cakes are completely cooled, place one layer on a serving plate. Spread a layer of frosting on top.
12. Place the second cake layer on top and frost the top and sides of the cake with the remaining frosting.
13. Optional: Decorate the cake with chocolate shavings, sprinkles, or additional frosting as desired.
14. Slice and serve your delicious old-fashioned chocolate cake. Enjoy!

Classic Lemon Bars

Ingredients:

For the crust:

- 1 cup all-purpose flour
- ½ cup unsalted butter, softened
- ¼ cup powdered sugar
- Pinch of salt

For the lemon filling:

- 1 ½ cups granulated sugar
- ¼ cup all-purpose flour
- 4 large eggs
- 2/3 cup freshly squeezed lemon juice (about 4-5 lemons)
- Zest of 2 lemons
- Powdered sugar, for dusting

Instructions:

1. Preheat your oven to 350°F (175°C). Grease a 9x13 inch baking pan or line it with parchment paper, leaving an overhang on the sides for easy removal.
2. In a mixing bowl, combine the flour, softened butter, powdered sugar, and salt for the crust. Mix until the dough comes together and resembles coarse crumbs.
3. Press the dough evenly into the bottom of the prepared baking pan.
4. Bake the crust in the preheated oven for 15-18 minutes, or until lightly golden brown.
5. While the crust is baking, prepare the lemon filling. In a separate bowl, whisk together the granulated sugar and flour.
6. Add the eggs, lemon juice, and lemon zest to the sugar mixture. Whisk until smooth and well combined.
7. Once the crust is baked, remove it from the oven and pour the lemon filling over the hot crust.
8. Return the pan to the oven and bake for an additional 20-25 minutes, or until the filling is set and the edges are lightly golden brown.
9. Remove the pan from the oven and allow the lemon bars to cool completely in the pan on a wire rack.
10. Once cooled, dust the top of the lemon bars with powdered sugar.
11. Use a sharp knife to cut the lemon bars into squares or rectangles.

12. Serve and enjoy these classic lemon bars! They can be stored in an airtight container in the refrigerator for up to 3 days.

Homemade Peach Cobbler

Ingredients:

For the peach filling:

- 6 cups fresh or frozen sliced peaches (about 6-8 peaches)
- 1 cup granulated sugar
- 2 tablespoons lemon juice
- 1 teaspoon pure vanilla extract
- 2 tablespoons cornstarch

For the cobbler topping:

- 1 ½ cups all-purpose flour
- 1 cup granulated sugar
- 1 teaspoon baking powder
- ½ teaspoon salt
- ¾ cup unsalted butter, melted
- 1 teaspoon pure vanilla extract
- ½ cup whole milk

Instructions:

1. Preheat your oven to 375°F (190°C). Grease a 9x13 inch baking dish or a similar-sized baking dish.
2. In a large mixing bowl, combine the sliced peaches, granulated sugar, lemon juice, vanilla extract, and cornstarch. Stir until the peaches are evenly coated. Let the mixture sit for about 10 minutes to allow the flavors to meld together.
3. Pour the peach mixture into the prepared baking dish, spreading it out evenly.
4. In another mixing bowl, whisk together the flour, granulated sugar, baking powder, and salt for the cobbler topping.
5. Stir in the melted butter, vanilla extract, and milk until a thick batter forms.
6. Spoon the batter evenly over the top of the peach mixture in the baking dish, spreading it out as evenly as possible.
7. Bake in the preheated oven for 40-45 minutes, or until the cobbler topping is golden brown and the peach filling is bubbly.

8. Remove the cobbler from the oven and let it cool for a few minutes before serving.
9. Serve warm, optionally with a scoop of vanilla ice cream or a dollop of whipped cream on top.
10. Enjoy your homemade peach cobbler! Any leftovers can be stored in an airtight container in the refrigerator for up to 3 days. Reheat before serving if desired.

Grandma's Blueberry Muffins

Ingredients:

- 2 cups all-purpose flour
- 1 tablespoon baking powder
- ½ teaspoon salt
- ½ cup unsalted butter, melted and cooled slightly
- 1 cup granulated sugar
- 2 large eggs
- 1 teaspoon pure vanilla extract
- ½ cup milk
- 1 ½ cups fresh or frozen blueberries
- Optional: Turbinado sugar for sprinkling on top

Instructions:

1. Preheat your oven to 375°F (190°C). Line a muffin tin with paper liners or grease the muffin cups.
2. In a large mixing bowl, sift together the flour, baking powder, and salt.
3. In a separate bowl, whisk together the melted butter and granulated sugar until well combined.
4. Add the eggs, one at a time, to the butter and sugar mixture, whisking well after each addition.
5. Stir in the vanilla extract.
6. Gradually add the flour mixture to the wet ingredients, alternating with the milk, beginning and ending with the flour mixture. Mix until just combined. Be careful not to overmix.
7. Gently fold in the blueberries until evenly distributed throughout the batter.
8. Divide the batter evenly among the prepared muffin cups, filling each about ¾ full.
9. Optional: Sprinkle the tops of the muffins with turbinado sugar for a crunchy topping.
10. Bake in the preheated oven for 18-20 minutes, or until the tops are golden brown and a toothpick inserted into the center of a muffin comes out clean.
11. Remove the muffins from the oven and let them cool in the pan for a few minutes before transferring them to a wire rack to cool completely.
12. Serve warm or at room temperature. Enjoy Grandma's delicious blueberry muffins! They can be stored in an airtight container at room temperature for up to 3 days.

Peanut Butter Cookies

Ingredients:

- 1 cup creamy peanut butter
- 1 cup granulated sugar
- 1 large egg
- 1 teaspoon pure vanilla extract
- Optional: Additional granulated sugar for rolling (for a crinkly top)

Instructions:

1. Preheat your oven to 350°F (175°C). Line a baking sheet with parchment paper or grease it lightly.
2. In a mixing bowl, combine the creamy peanut butter, granulated sugar, egg, and vanilla extract. Mix until well combined and smooth.
3. Optional: If desired, roll the dough into small balls, about 1 tablespoon each.
4. Place the dough balls on the prepared baking sheet, spacing them about 2 inches apart.
5. Using a fork, press down on each dough ball in a crisscross pattern to flatten slightly and create the classic peanut butter cookie pattern.
6. Optional: Sprinkle additional granulated sugar over the top of each cookie for a crinkly top.
7. Bake in the preheated oven for 10-12 minutes, or until the cookies are lightly golden brown around the edges.
8. Remove the baking sheet from the oven and let the cookies cool on the pan for a few minutes before transferring them to a wire rack to cool completely.
9. Once cooled, enjoy these classic peanut butter cookies with a glass of milk or your favorite beverage!
10. Store any leftovers in an airtight container at room temperature for up to 5 days. These cookies also freeze well for longer storage.

Butterscotch Pudding

Ingredients:

- 3/4 cup packed dark brown sugar
- 1/4 cup cornstarch
- 1/2 teaspoon salt
- 3 cups whole milk
- 3 large egg yolks
- 2 tablespoons unsalted butter
- 1 teaspoon pure vanilla extract
- Whipped cream, for serving (optional)

Instructions:

1. In a medium saucepan, whisk together the packed dark brown sugar, cornstarch, and salt until well combined.
2. Gradually whisk in the whole milk until smooth and there are no lumps.
3. Place the saucepan over medium heat and cook, stirring constantly, until the mixture thickens and comes to a boil, about 5-7 minutes.
4. Once the mixture boils, reduce the heat to low and cook for an additional 2 minutes, stirring constantly.
5. In a small bowl, lightly beat the egg yolks. Gradually whisk in about 1/2 cup of the hot pudding mixture to temper the eggs.
6. Pour the tempered egg mixture back into the saucepan with the remaining pudding mixture, whisking constantly to combine.
7. Continue to cook over low heat, stirring constantly, until the pudding thickens further, about 2-3 minutes.
8. Remove the saucepan from the heat and stir in the unsalted butter and pure vanilla extract until the butter is melted and the mixture is smooth.
9. Strain the pudding through a fine-mesh sieve into a clean bowl to remove any lumps or cooked egg bits (if any).
10. Divide the pudding among serving dishes or pour it into a large serving bowl.
11. Cover the surface of the pudding with plastic wrap to prevent a skin from forming. Chill in the refrigerator for at least 2 hours, or until completely chilled and set.
12. Serve the butterscotch pudding chilled, optionally topped with whipped cream, if desired.
13. Enjoy this rich and creamy butterscotch pudding as a delightful dessert!

Coconut Cream Pie

Ingredients:

For the pie crust:

- 1 ¼ cups all-purpose flour
- ½ teaspoon salt
- ½ cup unsalted butter, cold and cubed
- 3-4 tablespoons ice water

For the coconut custard filling:

- 1 cup sweetened shredded coconut
- 2 cups whole milk
- ½ cup granulated sugar
- 1/3 cup cornstarch
- 4 large egg yolks
- 2 tablespoons unsalted butter
- 1 teaspoon pure vanilla extract

For the whipped cream topping:

- 1 cup heavy cream
- 2 tablespoons powdered sugar
- ½ teaspoon pure vanilla extract
- Additional sweetened shredded coconut, toasted (for garnish)

Instructions:

1. To make the pie crust, in a large mixing bowl, combine the all-purpose flour and salt. Add the cold cubed butter and use a pastry cutter or fork to cut it into the flour until the mixture resembles coarse crumbs.
2. Gradually add the ice water, 1 tablespoon at a time, mixing with a fork until the dough comes together. Form the dough into a disk, wrap it in plastic wrap, and refrigerate for at least 1 hour.
3. Preheat your oven to 375°F (190°C). On a lightly floured surface, roll out the chilled dough into a circle about 12 inches in diameter. Transfer the dough to a 9-inch pie dish,

gently pressing it into the bottom and sides. Trim any excess dough and crimp the edges as desired.
4. Line the pie crust with parchment paper or aluminum foil and fill it with pie weights or dried beans. Bake in the preheated oven for 15 minutes. Remove the parchment paper and pie weights, then continue baking for an additional 10-15 minutes, or until the crust is golden brown. Remove from the oven and let cool completely.
5. To make the coconut custard filling, spread the sweetened shredded coconut in a single layer on a baking sheet. Toast in the preheated oven for 5-7 minutes, stirring occasionally, until golden brown. Set aside to cool.
6. In a saucepan, heat the whole milk over medium heat until it just begins to simmer.
7. In a separate mixing bowl, whisk together the granulated sugar, cornstarch, and egg yolks until smooth.
8. Gradually pour the hot milk into the egg mixture, whisking constantly to temper the eggs.
9. Return the mixture to the saucepan and cook over medium heat, stirring constantly, until thickened, about 5-7 minutes.
10. Remove the saucepan from the heat and stir in the toasted shredded coconut, unsalted butter, and pure vanilla extract until the butter is melted and the mixture is smooth.
11. Pour the coconut custard filling into the cooled pie crust, spreading it out evenly. Cover the surface with plastic wrap, making sure it touches the custard to prevent a skin from forming. Chill in the refrigerator for at least 4 hours, or until set.
12. To make the whipped cream topping, in a mixing bowl, beat the heavy cream, powdered sugar, and vanilla extract until stiff peaks form.
13. Spread the whipped cream over the chilled coconut custard filling. Optionally, garnish with additional toasted sweetened shredded coconut.
14. Slice and serve your delicious coconut cream pie. Enjoy!

Oatmeal Raisin Cookies

Ingredients:

- 1 cup unsalted butter, softened
- 1 cup packed light brown sugar
- 1/2 cup granulated sugar
- 2 large eggs
- 1 teaspoon pure vanilla extract
- 1 1/2 cups all-purpose flour
- 1 teaspoon baking soda
- 1 teaspoon ground cinnamon
- 1/2 teaspoon salt
- 3 cups old-fashioned rolled oats
- 1 cup raisins

Instructions:

1. Preheat your oven to 350°F (175°C). Line baking sheets with parchment paper or silicone baking mats.
2. In a large mixing bowl, cream together the softened unsalted butter, packed light brown sugar, and granulated sugar until light and fluffy.
3. Add the eggs, one at a time, beating well after each addition. Then, stir in the pure vanilla extract.
4. In a separate bowl, whisk together the all-purpose flour, baking soda, ground cinnamon, and salt.
5. Gradually add the dry ingredients to the wet ingredients, mixing until well combined.
6. Stir in the old-fashioned rolled oats until evenly distributed throughout the dough.
7. Gently fold in the raisins until they are evenly distributed in the dough.
8. Drop tablespoonfuls of dough onto the prepared baking sheets, spacing them about 2 inches apart.
9. Flatten each dough ball slightly with the back of a spoon or your fingers.
10. Bake in the preheated oven for 10-12 minutes, or until the cookies are golden brown around the edges.
11. Remove the cookies from the oven and let them cool on the baking sheets for a few minutes before transferring them to wire racks to cool completely.
12. Once cooled, store the oatmeal raisin cookies in an airtight container at room temperature for up to one week. Enjoy these delicious cookies with a glass of milk or your favorite beverage!

Banana Bread

Ingredients:

- 2 to 3 ripe bananas, mashed (about 1 cup)
- 1/3 cup unsalted butter, melted
- 3/4 cup granulated sugar
- 1 large egg, beaten
- 1 teaspoon pure vanilla extract
- 1 teaspoon baking soda
- Pinch of salt
- 1 1/2 cups all-purpose flour

Optional add-ins:

- 1/2 cup chopped nuts (such as walnuts or pecans)
- 1/2 cup chocolate chips
- 1/2 cup raisins or dried cranberries

Instructions:

1. Preheat your oven to 350°F (175°C). Grease a 9x5 inch loaf pan or line it with parchment paper.
2. In a large mixing bowl, mash the ripe bananas with a fork until smooth.
3. Stir in the melted unsalted butter.
4. Add the granulated sugar, beaten egg, and pure vanilla extract to the banana mixture, and mix until well combined.
5. Sprinkle the baking soda and salt over the mixture and stir until incorporated.
6. Gradually add the all-purpose flour to the wet ingredients, mixing until just combined. Be careful not to overmix.
7. If using any optional add-ins, fold them into the batter until evenly distributed.
8. Pour the batter into the prepared loaf pan, spreading it out evenly.
9. Bake in the preheated oven for 50-60 minutes, or until a toothpick inserted into the center comes out clean.
10. If the top of the bread starts to brown too quickly, you can tent it with aluminum foil halfway through baking.
11. Once baked, remove the banana bread from the oven and let it cool in the pan for 10 minutes.
12. After 10 minutes, transfer the bread to a wire rack to cool completely before slicing.

13. Slice and serve your delicious homemade banana bread. Enjoy it warm or at room temperature with a pat of butter, a drizzle of honey, or simply on its own!

Blackberry Crisp

Ingredients:

For the blackberry filling:

- 5 cups fresh blackberries
- 1/2 cup granulated sugar
- 2 tablespoons cornstarch
- 1 tablespoon lemon juice
- 1 teaspoon pure vanilla extract
- Zest of 1 lemon

For the crisp topping:

- 1 cup old-fashioned rolled oats
- 1/2 cup all-purpose flour
- 1/2 cup packed light brown sugar
- 1/2 teaspoon ground cinnamon
- 1/4 teaspoon salt
- 1/2 cup unsalted butter, melted

Instructions:

1. Preheat your oven to 375°F (190°C). Grease a 9x9 inch baking dish or a similar-sized baking dish.
2. In a large mixing bowl, combine the fresh blackberries, granulated sugar, cornstarch, lemon juice, pure vanilla extract, and lemon zest. Toss until the blackberries are evenly coated.
3. Pour the blackberry mixture into the prepared baking dish, spreading it out evenly.
4. In another mixing bowl, combine the old-fashioned rolled oats, all-purpose flour, packed light brown sugar, ground cinnamon, and salt for the crisp topping.
5. Stir in the melted unsalted butter until the mixture is crumbly and evenly moistened.
6. Sprinkle the crisp topping evenly over the blackberry filling in the baking dish.
7. Bake in the preheated oven for 30-35 minutes, or until the topping is golden brown and the blackberry filling is bubbling around the edges.
8. Remove the blackberry crisp from the oven and let it cool for a few minutes before serving.
9. Serve the blackberry crisp warm, optionally topped with a scoop of vanilla ice cream or a dollop of whipped cream.

10. Enjoy this delicious blackberry crisp as a comforting dessert!

Carrot Cake with Cream Cheese Frosting

Ingredients:

For the carrot cake:

- 2 cups all-purpose flour
- 2 teaspoons baking powder
- 1 1/2 teaspoons baking soda
- 1/2 teaspoon salt
- 2 teaspoons ground cinnamon
- 1/2 teaspoon ground nutmeg
- 1/2 teaspoon ground ginger
- 1 cup granulated sugar
- 1 cup packed light brown sugar
- 1 cup vegetable oil
- 4 large eggs
- 2 teaspoons pure vanilla extract
- 3 cups grated carrots (about 3-4 medium carrots)
- 1 cup chopped nuts (such as walnuts or pecans), optional
- 1/2 cup shredded coconut, optional
- 1/2 cup crushed pineapple, drained, optional

For the cream cheese frosting:

- 8 ounces cream cheese, softened
- 1/2 cup unsalted butter, softened
- 4 cups powdered sugar, sifted
- 2 teaspoons pure vanilla extract

Instructions:

1. Preheat your oven to 350°F (175°C). Grease and flour two 9-inch round cake pans or line them with parchment paper.
2. In a medium mixing bowl, sift together the all-purpose flour, baking powder, baking soda, salt, ground cinnamon, ground nutmeg, and ground ginger.
3. In a large mixing bowl, whisk together the granulated sugar, packed light brown sugar, vegetable oil, eggs, and pure vanilla extract until well combined.
4. Gradually add the dry ingredients to the wet ingredients, mixing until just combined.
5. Fold in the grated carrots until evenly distributed throughout the batter.

6. If using any optional add-ins such as chopped nuts, shredded coconut, or crushed pineapple, fold them into the batter at this point.
7. Divide the batter evenly between the prepared cake pans, spreading it out evenly.
8. Bake in the preheated oven for 25-30 minutes, or until a toothpick inserted into the center of the cakes comes out clean.
9. Remove the cakes from the oven and let them cool in the pans for 10 minutes before transferring them to wire racks to cool completely.
10. While the cakes are cooling, prepare the cream cheese frosting. In a large mixing bowl, beat the softened cream cheese and unsalted butter together until smooth and creamy.
11. Gradually add the sifted powdered sugar, one cup at a time, beating well after each addition.
12. Stir in the pure vanilla extract until well combined.
13. Once the cakes are completely cooled, place one cake layer on a serving plate or cake stand. Spread a layer of cream cheese frosting over the top.
14. Place the second cake layer on top and frost the top and sides of the cake with the remaining cream cheese frosting.
15. Optionally, garnish the top of the cake with chopped nuts or shredded carrots.
16. Chill the carrot cake in the refrigerator for at least 30 minutes before slicing and serving.
17. Serve and enjoy this delicious carrot cake with cream cheese frosting!

Snickerdoodle Cookies

Ingredients:

For the cookie dough:

- 1 cup unsalted butter, softened
- 1 1/2 cups granulated sugar
- 2 large eggs
- 1 teaspoon pure vanilla extract
- 2 3/4 cups all-purpose flour
- 2 teaspoons cream of tartar
- 1 teaspoon baking soda
- 1/2 teaspoon salt

For the cinnamon sugar coating:

- 1/4 cup granulated sugar
- 2 tablespoons ground cinnamon

Instructions:

1. Preheat your oven to 375°F (190°C). Line baking sheets with parchment paper or silicone baking mats.
2. In a large mixing bowl, cream together the softened unsalted butter and granulated sugar until light and fluffy.
3. Add the eggs, one at a time, beating well after each addition. Then, stir in the pure vanilla extract.
4. In a separate bowl, whisk together the all-purpose flour, cream of tartar, baking soda, and salt.
5. Gradually add the dry ingredients to the wet ingredients, mixing until just combined. Be careful not to overmix.
6. In a small bowl, mix together the granulated sugar and ground cinnamon for the cinnamon sugar coating.
7. Using a cookie scoop or your hands, shape the cookie dough into balls, about 1 inch in diameter.
8. Roll each dough ball in the cinnamon sugar mixture until evenly coated.

9. Place the coated dough balls onto the prepared baking sheets, spacing them about 2 inches apart.
10. Flatten each dough ball slightly with the bottom of a glass or your fingers.
11. Bake in the preheated oven for 8-10 minutes, or until the cookies are set and the edges are lightly golden brown.
12. Remove the cookies from the oven and let them cool on the baking sheets for a few minutes before transferring them to wire racks to cool completely.
13. Once cooled, store the snickerdoodle cookies in an airtight container at room temperature for up to one week. Enjoy these classic cookies with a glass of milk or your favorite beverage!

Pineapple Upside-Down Cake

Ingredients:

For the topping:

- 1/4 cup unsalted butter
- 2/3 cup packed light brown sugar
- 1 can (20 oz) pineapple slices in juice, drained
- Maraschino cherries, for garnish (optional)

For the cake batter:

- 1 1/2 cups all-purpose flour
- 1 teaspoon baking powder
- 1/4 teaspoon baking soda
- 1/4 teaspoon salt
- 1/2 cup unsalted butter, softened
- 3/4 cup granulated sugar
- 2 large eggs
- 1 teaspoon pure vanilla extract
- 1/2 cup sour cream or plain Greek yogurt
- 1/4 cup pineapple juice (reserved from the canned pineapple)

Instructions:

1. Preheat your oven to 350°F (175°C). Grease a 9-inch round cake pan or springform pan.
2. In a small saucepan, melt the 1/4 cup of unsalted butter over low heat. Once melted, pour it into the bottom of the prepared cake pan, spreading it out evenly.
3. Sprinkle the packed light brown sugar evenly over the melted butter in the pan.
4. Arrange the drained pineapple slices on top of the brown sugar in a single layer. You can place a maraschino cherry in the center of each pineapple ring if desired.
5. In a medium mixing bowl, sift together the all-purpose flour, baking powder, baking soda, and salt.
6. In a large mixing bowl, cream together the softened unsalted butter and granulated sugar until light and fluffy.
7. Add the eggs, one at a time, beating well after each addition. Then, stir in the pure vanilla extract.
8. Gradually add the dry ingredients to the wet ingredients, alternating with the sour cream or Greek yogurt, beginning and ending with the dry ingredients. Mix until just combined.

9. Stir in the reserved pineapple juice until evenly distributed throughout the batter.
10. Pour the batter over the pineapple slices in the prepared cake pan, spreading it out evenly.
11. Bake in the preheated oven for 35-40 minutes, or until a toothpick inserted into the center of the cake comes out clean.
12. Remove the cake from the oven and let it cool in the pan for 10 minutes.
13. After 10 minutes, carefully invert the cake onto a serving platter or cake stand. Let it cool slightly before slicing and serving.
14. Serve your delicious pineapple upside-down cake warm or at room temperature. Enjoy!

Grandma's Fudge Brownies

Ingredients:

For the topping:

- 1/4 cup unsalted butter
- 2/3 cup packed light brown sugar
- 1 can (20 oz) pineapple slices in juice, drained
- Maraschino cherries, for garnish (optional)

For the cake batter:

- 1 1/2 cups all-purpose flour
- 1 teaspoon baking powder
- 1/4 teaspoon baking soda
- 1/4 teaspoon salt
- 1/2 cup unsalted butter, softened
- 3/4 cup granulated sugar
- 2 large eggs
- 1 teaspoon pure vanilla extract
- 1/2 cup sour cream or plain Greek yogurt
- 1/4 cup pineapple juice (reserved from the canned pineapple)

Instructions:

1. Preheat your oven to 350°F (175°C). Grease a 9-inch round cake pan or springform pan.
2. In a small saucepan, melt the 1/4 cup of unsalted butter over low heat. Once melted, pour it into the bottom of the prepared cake pan, spreading it out evenly.
3. Sprinkle the packed light brown sugar evenly over the melted butter in the pan.
4. Arrange the drained pineapple slices on top of the brown sugar in a single layer. You can place a maraschino cherry in the center of each pineapple ring if desired.
5. In a medium mixing bowl, sift together the all-purpose flour, baking powder, baking soda, and salt.
6. In a large mixing bowl, cream together the softened unsalted butter and granulated sugar until light and fluffy.
7. Add the eggs, one at a time, beating well after each addition. Then, stir in the pure vanilla extract.
8. Gradually add the dry ingredients to the wet ingredients, alternating with the sour cream or Greek yogurt, beginning and ending with the dry ingredients. Mix until just combined.

9. Stir in the reserved pineapple juice until evenly distributed throughout the batter.
10. Pour the batter over the pineapple slices in the prepared cake pan, spreading it out evenly.
11. Bake in the preheated oven for 35-40 minutes, or until a toothpick inserted into the center of the cake comes out clean.
12. Remove the cake from the oven and let it cool in the pan for 10 minutes.
13. After 10 minutes, carefully invert the cake onto a serving platter or cake stand. Let it cool slightly before slicing and serving.
14. Serve your delicious pineapple upside-down cake warm or at room temperature. Enjoy!

Grandma's Fudge Brownies

Ingredients:

- 1 cup unsalted butter
- 2 cups granulated sugar
- 4 large eggs
- 1 teaspoon pure vanilla extract
- 1 cup all-purpose flour
- 3/4 cup unsweetened cocoa powder
- 1/2 teaspoon salt
- 1 cup chopped nuts (such as walnuts or pecans), optional

Instructions:

1. Preheat your oven to 350°F (175°C). Grease a 9x13 inch baking pan or line it with parchment paper.
2. In a medium saucepan, melt the unsalted butter over low heat. Once melted, remove from heat and let it cool slightly.
3. In a large mixing bowl, combine the granulated sugar, eggs, and pure vanilla extract. Beat with a hand mixer or whisk until well combined.
4. Slowly pour the melted butter into the egg mixture, stirring constantly until incorporated.
5. In a separate mixing bowl, sift together the all-purpose flour, unsweetened cocoa powder, and salt.
6. Gradually add the dry ingredients to the wet ingredients, stirring until just combined. Be careful not to overmix.
7. If using chopped nuts, fold them into the brownie batter until evenly distributed.
8. Pour the brownie batter into the prepared baking pan, spreading it out evenly.
9. Bake in the preheated oven for 25-30 minutes, or until a toothpick inserted into the center comes out with a few moist crumbs.
10. Remove the brownies from the oven and let them cool completely in the pan on a wire rack.
11. Once cooled, slice the brownies into squares and serve. Enjoy your Grandma's fudge brownies as a delightful treat!

Strawberry Rhubarb Pie

Ingredients:

For the pie crust:

- 2 1/2 cups all-purpose flour
- 1 teaspoon granulated sugar
- 1 teaspoon salt
- 1 cup unsalted butter, cold and cubed
- 6-8 tablespoons ice water

For the filling:

- 3 cups sliced rhubarb (about 1/2-inch thick slices)
- 3 cups sliced strawberries
- 1 cup granulated sugar
- 1/4 cup cornstarch
- 1 tablespoon lemon juice
- 1 teaspoon pure vanilla extract
- 1 tablespoon unsalted butter, cut into small pieces

For the egg wash (optional):

- 1 egg
- 1 tablespoon water

Instructions:

1. To make the pie crust, in a large mixing bowl, combine the all-purpose flour, granulated sugar, and salt. Add the cold cubed butter to the flour mixture.
2. Use a pastry cutter or fork to cut the butter into the flour until the mixture resembles coarse crumbs.
3. Gradually add the ice water, 1 tablespoon at a time, mixing with a fork until the dough comes together. Be careful not to overmix.
4. Divide the dough in half and shape each half into a disk. Wrap each disk in plastic wrap and refrigerate for at least 1 hour, or until firm.

5. Preheat your oven to 400°F (200°C). On a lightly floured surface, roll out one disk of the chilled dough into a circle about 12 inches in diameter. Transfer the rolled-out dough to a 9-inch pie dish, pressing it gently into the bottom and sides.
6. In a large mixing bowl, combine the sliced rhubarb, sliced strawberries, granulated sugar, cornstarch, lemon juice, and pure vanilla extract. Toss until the fruit is evenly coated.
7. Pour the fruit filling into the prepared pie crust, spreading it out evenly. Dot the top of the filling with the small pieces of unsalted butter.
8. Roll out the second disk of chilled dough into a circle about 12 inches in diameter. Place it over the fruit filling, or use strips of dough to create a lattice pattern.
9. Trim any excess dough from the edges and crimp the edges of the crust as desired.
10. If using an egg wash, whisk together the egg and water. Brush the top crust with the egg wash for a golden finish.
11. Place the pie on a baking sheet to catch any drips and bake in the preheated oven for 45-50 minutes, or until the crust is golden brown and the filling is bubbly.
12. Remove the pie from the oven and let it cool on a wire rack before slicing and serving.
13. Serve your delicious homemade strawberry rhubarb pie warm or at room temperature. Enjoy!

Classic Rice Pudding

Ingredients:

- 1/2 cup white rice (long-grain or medium-grain)
- 4 cups whole milk
- 1/2 cup granulated sugar
- 1/4 teaspoon salt
- 1 teaspoon pure vanilla extract
- 1/2 teaspoon ground cinnamon
- Optional toppings: Ground cinnamon, nutmeg, or raisins

Instructions:

1. Rinse the rice under cold water until the water runs clear. This removes excess starch from the rice.
2. In a medium saucepan, combine the rinsed rice and whole milk. Bring to a gentle boil over medium heat, stirring occasionally to prevent the rice from sticking to the bottom of the pan.
3. Once the mixture comes to a boil, reduce the heat to low and simmer, stirring occasionally, for about 25-30 minutes, or until the rice is tender and the mixture has thickened.
4. Stir in the granulated sugar, salt, pure vanilla extract, and ground cinnamon. Continue to cook for an additional 5-10 minutes, stirring occasionally, until the sugar is dissolved and the flavors are well combined.
5. Remove the saucepan from the heat and let the rice pudding cool slightly.
6. If desired, sprinkle ground cinnamon, nutmeg, or raisins over the top of the rice pudding before serving.
7. Serve the classic rice pudding warm or chilled, depending on your preference.
8. Enjoy this comforting and delicious dessert as a sweet treat any time of the day! Leftovers can be stored in the refrigerator for up to 3-4 days.

Molasses Cookies

Ingredients:

- 3/4 cup unsalted butter, softened
- 1 cup granulated sugar, plus extra for rolling
- 1/4 cup molasses
- 1 large egg
- 2 cups all-purpose flour
- 2 teaspoons baking soda
- 1/2 teaspoon ground cloves
- 1 teaspoon ground cinnamon
- 1/2 teaspoon ground ginger
- 1/4 teaspoon salt

Instructions:

1. Preheat your oven to 375°F (190°C). Line baking sheets with parchment paper or silicone baking mats.
2. In a large mixing bowl, cream together the softened unsalted butter and 1 cup of granulated sugar until light and fluffy.
3. Add the molasses and egg to the butter mixture, and beat until well combined.
4. In a separate mixing bowl, whisk together the all-purpose flour, baking soda, ground cloves, ground cinnamon, ground ginger, and salt.
5. Gradually add the dry ingredients to the wet ingredients, mixing until well combined and a dough forms.
6. Place some granulated sugar in a shallow bowl for rolling the cookie dough.
7. Roll the cookie dough into 1-inch balls, then roll each ball in the granulated sugar until coated.
8. Place the sugar-coated cookie dough balls on the prepared baking sheets, spacing them about 2 inches apart.
9. Flatten each dough ball slightly with the bottom of a glass or your fingers.
10. Bake in the preheated oven for 8-10 minutes, or until the cookies are set and the edges are lightly golden brown.
11. Remove the cookies from the oven and let them cool on the baking sheets for a few minutes before transferring them to wire racks to cool completely.
12. Once cooled, store the molasses cookies in an airtight container at room temperature for up to one week. Enjoy these deliciously spiced cookies with a glass of milk or your favorite beverage!

Raspberry Thumbprint Cookies

Ingredients:

- 1 cup unsalted butter, softened
- 2/3 cup granulated sugar
- 2 large egg yolks
- 1 teaspoon pure vanilla extract
- 2 cups all-purpose flour
- 1/2 teaspoon salt
- 1 cup raspberry jam or preserves

Instructions:

1. Preheat your oven to 375°F (190°C). Line baking sheets with parchment paper or silicone baking mats.
2. In a large mixing bowl, cream together the softened unsalted butter and granulated sugar until light and fluffy.
3. Add the egg yolks and pure vanilla extract to the butter mixture, and beat until well combined.
4. In a separate mixing bowl, whisk together the all-purpose flour and salt.
5. Gradually add the dry ingredients to the wet ingredients, mixing until a dough forms.
6. Roll the dough into 1-inch balls and place them on the prepared baking sheets, spacing them about 2 inches apart.
7. Use your thumb or the back of a small spoon to make an indentation in the center of each dough ball.
8. Fill each indentation with raspberry jam or preserves, about 1/2 teaspoon each.
9. Bake in the preheated oven for 10-12 minutes, or until the cookies are set and the edges are lightly golden brown.
10. Remove the cookies from the oven and let them cool on the baking sheets for a few minutes before transferring them to wire racks to cool completely.
11. Once cooled, store the raspberry thumbprint cookies in an airtight container at room temperature for up to one week. Enjoy these delightful cookies as a sweet treat!

Chocolate Chip Banana Bread

Ingredients:

- 2 cups all-purpose flour
- 1 teaspoon baking powder
- 1/2 teaspoon baking soda
- 1/2 teaspoon salt
- 1/2 cup unsalted butter, softened
- 1 cup granulated sugar
- 2 large eggs
- 3 ripe bananas, mashed (about 1 1/2 cups)
- 1 teaspoon pure vanilla extract
- 1 cup semi-sweet chocolate chips

Instructions:

1. Preheat your oven to 350°F (175°C). Grease a 9x5 inch loaf pan or line it with parchment paper.
2. In a medium mixing bowl, sift together the all-purpose flour, baking powder, baking soda, and salt.
3. In a large mixing bowl, cream together the softened unsalted butter and granulated sugar until light and fluffy.
4. Add the eggs, one at a time, to the butter mixture, beating well after each addition.
5. Stir in the mashed bananas and pure vanilla extract until well combined.
6. Gradually add the dry ingredients to the wet ingredients, mixing until just combined. Be careful not to overmix.
7. Fold in the semi-sweet chocolate chips until evenly distributed throughout the batter.
8. Pour the batter into the prepared loaf pan, spreading it out evenly.
9. Bake in the preheated oven for 60-70 minutes, or until a toothpick inserted into the center of the bread comes out clean.
10. If the top of the bread starts to brown too quickly, you can tent it with aluminum foil halfway through baking.
11. Remove the banana bread from the oven and let it cool in the pan for 10 minutes.
12. After 10 minutes, transfer the bread to a wire rack to cool completely before slicing and serving.
13. Serve your delicious chocolate chip banana bread slices warm or at room temperature. Enjoy as a breakfast treat or a tasty snack!

Old-Fashioned Bread Pudding

Ingredients:

- 6 cups stale bread, torn or cubed into 1-inch pieces (French bread, brioche, or challah work well)
- 2 cups whole milk
- 1 cup heavy cream
- 3/4 cup granulated sugar
- 4 large eggs
- 1 teaspoon pure vanilla extract
- 1/2 teaspoon ground cinnamon
- 1/4 teaspoon ground nutmeg
- 1/4 teaspoon salt
- 1/2 cup raisins or dried cranberries (optional)
- Whipped cream or vanilla ice cream, for serving (optional)

Instructions:

1. Preheat your oven to 350°F (175°C). Grease a 9x13 inch baking dish or similar-sized casserole dish.
2. Place the torn or cubed stale bread pieces in a large mixing bowl.
3. In a separate saucepan, heat the whole milk and heavy cream over medium heat until it just begins to simmer. Remove from heat.
4. In a mixing bowl, whisk together the granulated sugar, eggs, pure vanilla extract, ground cinnamon, ground nutmeg, and salt until well combined.
5. Gradually pour the hot milk and cream mixture into the egg mixture, whisking constantly to temper the eggs.
6. Pour the custard mixture over the bread pieces in the mixing bowl. Add the raisins or dried cranberries, if using. Gently stir until all the bread pieces are coated and soaked in the custard.
7. Let the mixture sit for about 10-15 minutes to allow the bread to absorb the custard.
8. Transfer the bread pudding mixture to the prepared baking dish, spreading it out evenly.
9. Place the baking dish in a larger roasting pan or baking dish. Pour hot water into the larger pan to create a water bath, coming halfway up the sides of the baking dish.
10. Bake in the preheated oven for 45-55 minutes, or until the bread pudding is set and golden brown on top.
11. Remove the bread pudding from the oven and let it cool slightly before serving.
12. Serve the old-fashioned bread pudding warm, optionally topped with whipped cream or vanilla ice cream. Enjoy this comforting dessert!

Grandma's Pound Cake

Ingredients:

- 1 cup unsalted butter, softened
- 2 cups granulated sugar
- 4 large eggs
- 1 teaspoon pure vanilla extract
- 3 cups all-purpose flour
- 1/2 teaspoon baking powder
- 1/2 teaspoon salt
- 1 cup whole milk

Instructions:

1. Preheat your oven to 325°F (160°C). Grease and flour a 10-inch tube or bundt pan.
2. In a large mixing bowl, cream together the softened unsalted butter and granulated sugar until light and fluffy.
3. Add the eggs one at a time, beating well after each addition. Then, stir in the pure vanilla extract.
4. In a separate mixing bowl, sift together the all-purpose flour, baking powder, and salt.
5. Gradually add the dry ingredients to the wet ingredients, alternating with the whole milk, beginning and ending with the dry ingredients. Mix until just combined. Be careful not to overmix.
6. Pour the batter into the prepared tube or bundt pan, spreading it out evenly.
7. Bake in the preheated oven for 60-70 minutes, or until a toothpick inserted into the center of the cake comes out clean.
8. If the top of the cake starts to brown too quickly, you can tent it with aluminum foil halfway through baking.
9. Remove the cake from the oven and let it cool in the pan for about 10 minutes.
10. After 10 minutes, carefully invert the cake onto a wire rack to cool completely.
11. Once cooled, slice and serve your delicious Grandma's pound cake. Enjoy it plain or with your favorite toppings, such as fresh fruit or whipped cream!

Buttermilk Biscuits with Strawberry Jam

Ingredients:

For the biscuits:

- 2 cups all-purpose flour
- 1 tablespoon granulated sugar
- 1 tablespoon baking powder
- 1/2 teaspoon baking soda
- 1/2 teaspoon salt
- 1/2 cup unsalted butter, cold and cut into small pieces
- 3/4 cup buttermilk, cold

For serving:

- Strawberry jam or preserves

Instructions:

1. Preheat your oven to 425°F (220°C). Line a baking sheet with parchment paper or lightly grease it.
2. In a large mixing bowl, sift together the all-purpose flour, granulated sugar, baking powder, baking soda, and salt.
3. Add the cold, cubed unsalted butter to the flour mixture. Use a pastry cutter or your fingertips to quickly work the butter into the flour until the mixture resembles coarse crumbs.
4. Make a well in the center of the flour mixture and pour in the cold buttermilk. Stir the mixture with a fork or spatula until the dough just comes together. Be careful not to overmix.
5. Turn the dough out onto a lightly floured surface and gently knead it a few times until it holds together.
6. Pat the dough into a circle about 1/2 to 3/4 inch thick. Use a round biscuit cutter or a glass dipped in flour to cut out biscuits. Press straight down without twisting to ensure the biscuits rise evenly.
7. Place the biscuits on the prepared baking sheet, leaving a little space between each one.
8. Bake in the preheated oven for 12-15 minutes, or until the biscuits are golden brown on top and cooked through.
9. Remove the biscuits from the oven and let them cool on a wire rack for a few minutes.

10. Serve the warm buttermilk biscuits with strawberry jam or preserves.
11. Enjoy these delicious buttermilk biscuits with strawberry jam as a delightful breakfast or snack!

Peach Pie

Ingredients:

For the crust:

- 2 1/2 cups all-purpose flour
- 1 teaspoon salt
- 1 cup unsalted butter, cold and cut into small pieces
- 6-8 tablespoons ice water

For the filling:

- 6-7 cups sliced peeled peaches (about 6-8 medium peaches)
- 1/2 cup granulated sugar
- 1/4 cup packed light brown sugar
- 1/4 cup all-purpose flour
- 1 tablespoon lemon juice
- 1/2 teaspoon ground cinnamon
- 1/4 teaspoon ground nutmeg
- 1/4 teaspoon salt

For the topping:

- 2 tablespoons unsalted butter, cut into small pieces
- 1 tablespoon granulated sugar

Instructions:

1. Preheat your oven to 400°F (200°C).
2. In a large mixing bowl, combine the sliced peeled peaches, granulated sugar, brown sugar, all-purpose flour, lemon juice, ground cinnamon, ground nutmeg, and salt. Toss until the peaches are evenly coated with the sugar mixture. Set aside.
3. In another mixing bowl, prepare the pie crust. Mix together the all-purpose flour and salt. Add the cold, cubed unsalted butter and use a pastry cutter or your fingertips to work the butter into the flour until the mixture resembles coarse crumbs. Gradually add the ice water, one tablespoon at a time, mixing until the dough comes together.

4. Divide the dough into two equal parts. Roll out one part of the dough on a lightly floured surface to fit a 9-inch pie dish. Place the rolled-out dough into the pie dish, trimming any excess dough from the edges.
5. Pour the peach filling into the prepared pie crust, spreading it out evenly.
6. Dot the top of the peach filling with the small pieces of unsalted butter.
7. Roll out the remaining dough on a lightly floured surface to fit the top of the pie. Place the rolled-out dough over the peach filling. Trim any excess dough from the edges and crimp the edges of the crust to seal.
8. Use a sharp knife to make a few small slits in the top crust to allow steam to escape during baking.
9. Sprinkle the top of the pie with granulated sugar.
10. Place the pie on a baking sheet to catch any drips and bake in the preheated oven for 45-50 minutes, or until the crust is golden brown and the filling is bubbling.
11. If the edges of the crust start to brown too quickly, you can cover them with aluminum foil halfway through baking.
12. Once baked, remove the pie from the oven and let it cool on a wire rack for at least 1 hour before slicing and serving.
13. Serve your delicious peach pie warm or at room temperature, optionally topped with a scoop of vanilla ice cream or a dollop of whipped cream. Enjoy!

Lemon Meringue Pie

Ingredients:

For the crust:

- 1 1/4 cups all-purpose flour
- 1/2 teaspoon salt
- 1/2 cup unsalted butter, cold and cut into small pieces
- 4-6 tablespoons ice water

For the lemon filling:

- 1 cup granulated sugar
- 1/4 cup cornstarch
- 1/4 teaspoon salt
- 1 1/2 cups water
- 4 large egg yolks
- 1 tablespoon lemon zest
- 1/2 cup fresh lemon juice
- 2 tablespoons unsalted butter

For the meringue:

- 4 large egg whites, at room temperature
- 1/4 teaspoon cream of tartar
- 1/2 cup granulated sugar
- 1/2 teaspoon vanilla extract

Instructions:

1. Preheat your oven to 350°F (175°C).
2. In a large mixing bowl, combine the all-purpose flour and salt. Add the cold, cubed unsalted butter and use a pastry cutter or your fingertips to work the butter into the flour until the mixture resembles coarse crumbs. Gradually add the ice water, one tablespoon at a time, mixing until the dough comes together.
3. Form the dough into a ball, flatten it into a disk, and wrap it in plastic wrap. Chill the dough in the refrigerator for at least 30 minutes.

4. Once chilled, roll out the dough on a lightly floured surface to fit a 9-inch pie dish. Place the rolled-out dough into the pie dish, trimming any excess dough from the edges. Crimp the edges of the crust as desired.
5. Use a fork to prick the bottom and sides of the crust to prevent air bubbles from forming during baking. Line the crust with parchment paper or aluminum foil and fill it with pie weights or dried beans.
6. Blind bake the crust in the preheated oven for 15 minutes. Remove the parchment paper and pie weights, and continue to bake for another 10-15 minutes, or until the crust is golden brown. Remove from the oven and let it cool while you prepare the filling.
7. In a medium saucepan, whisk together the granulated sugar, cornstarch, and salt. Gradually whisk in the water until smooth. Place the saucepan over medium heat and cook, stirring constantly, until the mixture comes to a boil and thickens.
8. In a separate mixing bowl, whisk the egg yolks until smooth. Gradually whisk in about half of the hot sugar mixture to temper the eggs, then pour the egg mixture back into the saucepan with the remaining sugar mixture, whisking constantly.
9. Cook the mixture over medium heat, stirring constantly, until it thickens to a pudding-like consistency, about 2-3 minutes.
10. Remove from heat and stir in the lemon zest, lemon juice, and unsalted butter until the butter is melted and the mixture is smooth.
11. Pour the lemon filling into the pre-baked pie crust, spreading it out evenly.
12. In a clean mixing bowl, beat the egg whites with an electric mixer on medium speed until foamy. Add the cream of tartar and continue to beat until soft peaks form.
13. Gradually add the granulated sugar, about a tablespoon at a time, while continuing to beat on high speed, until stiff peaks form. Beat in the vanilla extract.
14. Spread the meringue over the hot lemon filling, making sure to seal the edges of the pie crust to prevent shrinking.
15. Use the back of a spoon to create peaks in the meringue.
16. Bake the pie in the preheated oven for 10-12 minutes, or until the meringue is golden brown.
17. Remove from the oven and let it cool completely on a wire rack.
18. Once cooled, refrigerate the pie for at least 4 hours, or until the filling is set.
19. Slice and serve your delicious lemon meringue pie. Enjoy this classic dessert with its tangy lemon filling and fluffy meringue topping!

Cinnamon Rolls

Ingredients:

For the dough:

- 1 cup warm milk (110°F/45°C)
- 2 1/4 teaspoons active dry yeast (1 packet)
- 1/2 cup granulated sugar
- 1/3 cup unsalted butter, melted
- 2 large eggs
- 4 1/2 cups all-purpose flour
- 1 teaspoon salt

For the filling:

- 1/3 cup unsalted butter, softened
- 1 cup packed brown sugar
- 2 1/2 tablespoons ground cinnamon

For the cream cheese icing:

- 4 ounces cream cheese, softened
- 1/4 cup unsalted butter, softened
- 1 cup powdered sugar
- 1/2 teaspoon vanilla extract
- 2-3 tablespoons milk (adjust to desired consistency)

Instructions:

1. In a small bowl, dissolve the active dry yeast in warm milk and let it sit for about 5 minutes until frothy.
2. In a large mixing bowl or the bowl of a stand mixer, combine the dissolved yeast mixture, granulated sugar, melted butter, eggs, flour, and salt. Mix until well combined and a soft dough forms.
3. Knead the dough on a floured surface or using a dough hook attachment in a stand mixer for about 5-7 minutes until it becomes smooth and elastic.

4. Place the dough in a greased bowl, cover it with a clean kitchen towel or plastic wrap, and let it rise in a warm place for about 1-1.5 hours or until doubled in size.
5. Once the dough has doubled in size, punch it down to release the air.
6. Roll out the dough on a floured surface into a large rectangle, about 16x20 inches in size.
7. Spread the softened butter evenly over the rolled-out dough, leaving a small border around the edges.
8. In a small bowl, mix together the brown sugar and ground cinnamon. Sprinkle the cinnamon sugar mixture evenly over the buttered dough.
9. Starting from one long edge, tightly roll up the dough into a log. Pinch the seam to seal.
10. Use a sharp knife to slice the rolled-up dough into 12 equal-sized pieces.
11. Place the cinnamon rolls in a greased 9x13 inch baking dish or two 9-inch round cake pans, spacing them evenly.
12. Cover the baking dish with a clean kitchen towel or plastic wrap and let the cinnamon rolls rise in a warm place for about 30-45 minutes, or until they have doubled in size.
13. Preheat your oven to 350°F (175°C).
14. Once the cinnamon rolls have risen, bake them in the preheated oven for 20-25 minutes, or until they are golden brown and cooked through.
15. While the cinnamon rolls are baking, prepare the cream cheese icing. In a mixing bowl, beat together the softened cream cheese and butter until smooth. Gradually add the powdered sugar and vanilla extract, mixing until well combined. Add milk, 1 tablespoon at a time, until the icing reaches your desired consistency.
16. Remove the cinnamon rolls from the oven and let them cool in the baking dish for a few minutes.
17. Spread the cream cheese icing over the warm cinnamon rolls.
18. Serve the cinnamon rolls warm and enjoy!

Homemade Strawberry Shortcake

Ingredients:

For the shortcakes:

- 2 cups all-purpose flour
- 1/4 cup granulated sugar
- 1 tablespoon baking powder
- 1/2 teaspoon salt
- 1/2 cup unsalted butter, cold and cut into small pieces
- 3/4 cup milk
- 1 teaspoon vanilla extract

For the strawberries:

- 4 cups fresh strawberries, hulled and sliced
- 1/4 cup granulated sugar
- 1 tablespoon lemon juice

For the whipped cream:

- 1 cup heavy cream, chilled
- 2 tablespoons powdered sugar
- 1 teaspoon vanilla extract

Instructions:

1. Preheat your oven to 425°F (220°C). Line a baking sheet with parchment paper or lightly grease it.
2. In a large mixing bowl, whisk together the all-purpose flour, granulated sugar, baking powder, and salt.
3. Add the cold, cubed unsalted butter to the flour mixture. Use a pastry cutter or your fingertips to work the butter into the flour until the mixture resembles coarse crumbs.
4. In a separate measuring cup, combine the milk and vanilla extract. Gradually add the milk mixture to the flour mixture, stirring until the dough comes together.
5. Turn the dough out onto a lightly floured surface and gently knead it a few times until it holds together.

6. Pat the dough into a circle about 3/4 inch thick. Use a round biscuit cutter or a glass dipped in flour to cut out shortcakes. Place the shortcakes onto the prepared baking sheet.
7. Bake in the preheated oven for 12-15 minutes, or until the shortcakes are golden brown on top.
8. While the shortcakes are baking, prepare the strawberries. In a mixing bowl, toss together the sliced strawberries, granulated sugar, and lemon juice. Let the strawberries macerate while the shortcakes bake.
9. In another mixing bowl, prepare the whipped cream. Using a hand mixer or stand mixer, whip the chilled heavy cream, powdered sugar, and vanilla extract until stiff peaks form.
10. Once the shortcakes are baked and cooled slightly, split them in half horizontally.
11. To assemble, place a spoonful of macerated strawberries on the bottom half of each shortcake. Top with a dollop of whipped cream, then place the other half of the shortcake on top.
12. Serve the homemade strawberry shortcakes immediately and enjoy this classic dessert!

Grandma's Chocolate Chip Cookies

Ingredients:

- 2 1/4 cups all-purpose flour
- 1 teaspoon baking soda
- 1/2 teaspoon salt
- 1 cup unsalted butter, softened
- 3/4 cup granulated sugar
- 3/4 cup packed brown sugar
- 1 teaspoon vanilla extract
- 2 large eggs
- 2 cups semisweet chocolate chips

Instructions:

1. Preheat your oven to 375°F (190°C). Line baking sheets with parchment paper or silicone baking mats.
2. In a medium mixing bowl, whisk together the all-purpose flour, baking soda, and salt. Set aside.
3. In a large mixing bowl, cream together the softened unsalted butter, granulated sugar, and brown sugar until light and fluffy.
4. Beat in the vanilla extract and eggs, one at a time, until well combined.
5. Gradually add the dry ingredients to the wet ingredients, mixing until just combined.
6. Stir in the semisweet chocolate chips until evenly distributed throughout the cookie dough.
7. Drop rounded tablespoons of dough onto the prepared baking sheets, spacing them about 2 inches apart.
8. Bake in the preheated oven for 9-11 minutes, or until the cookies are golden brown around the edges.
9. Remove the cookies from the oven and let them cool on the baking sheets for a few minutes before transferring them to wire racks to cool completely.
10. Once cooled, store the Grandma's chocolate chip cookies in an airtight container at room temperature. Enjoy these classic cookies with a glass of milk or your favorite beverage!

Blueberry Buckle

Ingredients:

For the streusel topping:

- 1/2 cup all-purpose flour
- 1/2 cup granulated sugar
- 1/2 teaspoon ground cinnamon
- 1/4 cup unsalted butter, cold and cut into small pieces

For the cake:

- 2 cups all-purpose flour
- 2 teaspoons baking powder
- 1/2 teaspoon salt
- 1/2 cup unsalted butter, softened
- 3/4 cup granulated sugar
- 2 large eggs
- 1 teaspoon vanilla extract
- 1/2 cup milk
- 2 cups fresh or frozen blueberries

Instructions:

1. Preheat your oven to 375°F (190°C). Grease a 9-inch square baking pan or a 9-inch round cake pan.
2. To make the streusel topping, in a small mixing bowl, combine the all-purpose flour, granulated sugar, and ground cinnamon. Cut in the cold, cubed unsalted butter using a pastry cutter or your fingertips until the mixture resembles coarse crumbs. Set aside.
3. In a medium mixing bowl, whisk together the all-purpose flour, baking powder, and salt. Set aside.
4. In a large mixing bowl, cream together the softened unsalted butter and granulated sugar until light and fluffy.
5. Beat in the eggs, one at a time, until well combined. Stir in the vanilla extract.
6. Gradually add the dry ingredients to the wet ingredients, alternating with the milk, beginning and ending with the dry ingredients. Mix until just combined.
7. Gently fold in the blueberries until evenly distributed throughout the batter.
8. Spread the batter evenly into the prepared baking pan.
9. Sprinkle the streusel topping evenly over the top of the batter.

10. Bake in the preheated oven for 35-40 minutes, or until a toothpick inserted into the center comes out clean and the streusel topping is golden brown.
11. Remove the blueberry buckle from the oven and let it cool in the pan for about 10 minutes.
12. Serve the blueberry buckle warm or at room temperature. Enjoy this delicious coffee cake-like treat for breakfast or dessert!

Cherry Crisp

Ingredients:

For the cherry filling:

- 4 cups pitted fresh or frozen cherries
- 1/2 cup granulated sugar
- 2 tablespoons cornstarch
- 1 tablespoon lemon juice
- 1/2 teaspoon vanilla extract

For the crisp topping:

- 3/4 cup old-fashioned rolled oats
- 1/2 cup all-purpose flour
- 1/2 cup packed brown sugar
- 1/4 teaspoon salt
- 1/2 teaspoon ground cinnamon
- 1/3 cup unsalted butter, melted

Instructions:

1. Preheat your oven to 375°F (190°C). Grease a 9-inch square baking dish or similar-sized baking dish.
2. In a large mixing bowl, combine the pitted cherries, granulated sugar, cornstarch, lemon juice, and vanilla extract. Stir until the cherries are well coated with the sugar mixture.
3. Transfer the cherry filling to the prepared baking dish, spreading it out evenly.
4. In another mixing bowl, combine the old-fashioned rolled oats, all-purpose flour, brown sugar, salt, and ground cinnamon. Mix until well combined.
5. Pour the melted unsalted butter over the oat mixture and stir until the mixture is evenly moistened and crumbly.
6. Sprinkle the oat mixture evenly over the cherry filling in the baking dish.
7. Bake in the preheated oven for 30-35 minutes, or until the cherry filling is bubbly and the crisp topping is golden brown.
8. Remove the cherry crisp from the oven and let it cool slightly before serving.
9. Serve the cherry crisp warm, optionally topped with a scoop of vanilla ice cream or a dollop of whipped cream.
10. Enjoy this delightful cherry dessert!

Apple Crumble

Ingredients:

For the apple filling:

- 6 cups peeled, cored, and sliced apples (such as Granny Smith or Honeycrisp)
- 1/4 cup granulated sugar
- 2 tablespoons all-purpose flour
- 1 teaspoon ground cinnamon
- 1/4 teaspoon ground nutmeg
- 1 tablespoon lemon juice
- 1 teaspoon vanilla extract

For the crumble topping:

- 1 cup old-fashioned rolled oats
- 1/2 cup all-purpose flour
- 1/2 cup packed brown sugar
- 1/4 teaspoon salt
- 1/2 teaspoon ground cinnamon
- 1/2 cup unsalted butter, cold and cut into small pieces

Instructions:

1. Preheat your oven to 375°F (190°C). Grease a 9-inch square baking dish or similar-sized baking dish.
2. In a large mixing bowl, combine the sliced apples, granulated sugar, all-purpose flour, ground cinnamon, ground nutmeg, lemon juice, and vanilla extract. Toss until the apples are well coated with the sugar mixture.
3. Transfer the apple filling to the prepared baking dish, spreading it out evenly.
4. In another mixing bowl, combine the old-fashioned rolled oats, all-purpose flour, brown sugar, salt, and ground cinnamon. Mix until well combined.
5. Add the cold, cubed unsalted butter to the oat mixture. Use a pastry cutter or your fingertips to work the butter into the mixture until it resembles coarse crumbs.
6. Sprinkle the crumble topping evenly over the apple filling in the baking dish.
7. Bake in the preheated oven for 35-40 minutes, or until the apple filling is bubbling and the crumble topping is golden brown.
8. Remove the apple crumble from the oven and let it cool slightly before serving.

9. Serve the apple crumble warm, optionally topped with a scoop of vanilla ice cream or a dollop of whipped cream.
10. Enjoy this comforting dessert with the perfect balance of sweet, tart, and crunchy flavors!

Date Squares

Ingredients:

For the date filling:

- 2 cups pitted dates, chopped
- 1 cup water
- 1/4 cup granulated sugar
- 1 tablespoon lemon juice
- 1/2 teaspoon vanilla extract

For the oatmeal crust and topping:

- 1 1/2 cups old-fashioned rolled oats
- 1 1/2 cups all-purpose flour
- 1 cup packed brown sugar
- 1/2 teaspoon baking soda
- 1/4 teaspoon salt
- 1 cup unsalted butter, softened

Instructions:

1. Preheat your oven to 350°F (175°C). Grease a 9x9-inch baking pan or line it with parchment paper, leaving some overhang for easy removal.
2. In a medium saucepan, combine the chopped dates, water, granulated sugar, lemon juice, and vanilla extract. Bring the mixture to a simmer over medium heat, stirring occasionally. Reduce the heat to low and simmer for about 5-7 minutes, or until the dates are soft and the mixture has thickened. Remove from heat and let it cool slightly.
3. In a large mixing bowl, combine the old-fashioned rolled oats, all-purpose flour, packed brown sugar, baking soda, and salt. Mix until well combined.
4. Add the softened unsalted butter to the oat mixture. Use your hands or a pastry cutter to work the butter into the dry ingredients until the mixture resembles coarse crumbs.
5. Press half of the oat mixture evenly into the bottom of the prepared baking pan.
6. Spread the date filling evenly over the oat crust in the baking pan.
7. Sprinkle the remaining oat mixture evenly over the date filling, pressing it down gently.
8. Bake in the preheated oven for 25-30 minutes, or until the top is golden brown.
9. Remove the date squares from the oven and let them cool completely in the pan on a wire rack.

10. Once cooled, use the parchment paper overhang to lift the date squares out of the pan. Place them on a cutting board and cut into squares or bars.
11. Serve the date squares at room temperature and enjoy this classic treat with a cup of tea or coffee!

Shortbread Cookies

Ingredients:

- 1 cup (2 sticks) unsalted butter, at room temperature
- 1/2 cup granulated sugar
- 2 cups all-purpose flour
- 1/4 teaspoon salt
- Optional: 1 teaspoon vanilla extract or other flavoring (such as almond extract or lemon zest)

Instructions:

1. Preheat your oven to 350°F (175°C). Line a baking sheet with parchment paper or lightly grease it.
2. In a large mixing bowl, cream together the room temperature unsalted butter and granulated sugar until smooth and creamy.
3. Add the all-purpose flour and salt to the butter mixture. If using, add the vanilla extract or other flavoring.
4. Mix everything together until a soft dough forms. Be careful not to overmix.
5. Transfer the dough onto a lightly floured surface. Gently knead the dough a few times until it comes together.
6. Roll out the dough to about 1/4 inch (0.6 cm) thickness.
7. Use cookie cutters to cut out shapes from the dough. Alternatively, you can use a sharp knife to cut the dough into squares or rectangles.
8. Place the cut-out cookies onto the prepared baking sheet, leaving a little space between each cookie.
9. Prick each cookie with a fork or toothpick to create decorative holes.
10. Bake in the preheated oven for 12-15 minutes, or until the edges of the cookies are lightly golden brown.
11. Remove the cookies from the oven and let them cool on the baking sheet for a few minutes before transferring them to a wire rack to cool completely.
12. Once cooled, store the shortbread cookies in an airtight container at room temperature. Enjoy these buttery delights with a cup of tea or coffee!

Coconut Macaroons

Ingredients:

- 4 large egg whites
- 1/2 cup granulated sugar
- 1/4 teaspoon salt
- 1 teaspoon vanilla extract
- 3 cups shredded sweetened coconut

Instructions:

1. Preheat your oven to 325°F (160°C). Line a baking sheet with parchment paper or a silicone baking mat.
2. In a clean, dry mixing bowl, beat the egg whites until they reach soft peaks.
3. Gradually add the granulated sugar and salt to the egg whites while continuing to beat. Beat until stiff peaks form.
4. Gently fold in the vanilla extract and shredded sweetened coconut until well combined.
5. Drop rounded tablespoons of the coconut mixture onto the prepared baking sheet, spacing them about 1 inch apart.
6. Bake in the preheated oven for 20-25 minutes, or until the coconut macaroons are lightly golden brown on the edges and set.
7. Remove the baking sheet from the oven and let the macaroons cool on the baking sheet for a few minutes before transferring them to a wire rack to cool completely.
8. Once cooled, store the coconut macaroons in an airtight container at room temperature.
9. Enjoy these sweet and chewy coconut treats as a delightful snack or dessert!

Grandma's Gingerbread Cake

Ingredients:

- 1/2 cup unsalted butter, softened
- 1/2 cup granulated sugar
- 1/2 cup molasses
- 1 large egg
- 1 1/2 cups all-purpose flour
- 1 teaspoon baking soda
- 1/2 teaspoon salt
- 1 teaspoon ground ginger
- 1 teaspoon ground cinnamon
- 1/4 teaspoon ground cloves
- 3/4 cup hot water

Instructions:

1. Preheat your oven to 350°F (175°C). Grease and flour an 8-inch square baking pan.
2. In a large mixing bowl, cream together the softened unsalted butter and granulated sugar until light and fluffy.
3. Beat in the molasses and egg until well combined.
4. In a separate mixing bowl, sift together the all-purpose flour, baking soda, salt, ground ginger, ground cinnamon, and ground cloves.
5. Gradually add the dry ingredients to the wet ingredients, mixing until well combined.
6. Gradually stir in the hot water until the batter is smooth.
7. Pour the batter into the prepared baking pan, spreading it out evenly.
8. Bake in the preheated oven for 30-35 minutes, or until a toothpick inserted into the center comes out clean.
9. Remove the gingerbread cake from the oven and let it cool in the pan for about 10 minutes.
10. Once cooled slightly, remove the cake from the pan and transfer it to a wire rack to cool completely.
11. Serve the gingerbread cake plain or with a dollop of whipped cream or vanilla ice cream, if desired.

12. Enjoy Grandma's gingerbread cake as a delicious dessert or snack, especially during the holiday season!

Pecan Pie Bars

Ingredients:

For the crust:

- 1 1/2 cups all-purpose flour
- 1/2 cup confectioners' sugar
- 3/4 cup unsalted butter, cold and cubed

For the pecan filling:

- 3/4 cup unsalted butter
- 1 cup packed brown sugar
- 1/2 cup honey or corn syrup
- 2 tablespoons heavy cream
- 1/4 teaspoon salt
- 2 cups chopped pecans
- 1 teaspoon vanilla extract

Instructions:

1. Preheat your oven to 350°F (175°C). Grease or line a 9x13-inch baking pan with parchment paper, leaving some overhang for easy removal.
2. In a medium mixing bowl, combine the all-purpose flour and confectioners' sugar. Cut in the cold, cubed unsalted butter using a pastry cutter or your fingertips until the mixture resembles coarse crumbs.
3. Press the mixture evenly into the bottom of the prepared baking pan to form the crust. Bake in the preheated oven for 15-20 minutes, or until lightly golden brown.
4. While the crust is baking, prepare the pecan filling. In a medium saucepan, melt the unsalted butter over medium heat. Stir in the packed brown sugar, honey or corn syrup, heavy cream, and salt. Bring the mixture to a boil, stirring constantly.
5. Remove the saucepan from the heat and stir in the chopped pecans and vanilla extract until well combined.
6. Pour the pecan filling over the hot crust, spreading it out evenly.
7. Return the baking pan to the oven and bake for an additional 20-25 minutes, or until the filling is bubbly and set.
8. Remove the pecan pie bars from the oven and let them cool completely in the pan on a wire rack.

9. Once cooled, use the parchment paper overhang to lift the pecan pie bars out of the pan. Place them on a cutting board and cut into squares or bars.
10. Serve the pecan pie bars at room temperature and enjoy this decadent treat as a dessert or snack!

Buttermilk Pancakes with Maple Syrup

Ingredients:

- 1 1/2 cups all-purpose flour
- 3 1/2 teaspoons baking powder
- 1 teaspoon salt
- 1 tablespoon granulated sugar
- 1 1/4 cups buttermilk
- 1 large egg
- 3 tablespoons unsalted butter, melted
- Butter or oil for greasing the skillet
- Maple syrup for serving

Instructions:

1. In a large mixing bowl, sift together the all-purpose flour, baking powder, salt, and granulated sugar.
2. In a separate mixing bowl, whisk together the buttermilk, egg, and melted unsalted butter until well combined.
3. Pour the wet ingredients into the dry ingredients and stir until just combined. Be careful not to overmix; it's okay if the batter is slightly lumpy.
4. Heat a non-stick skillet or griddle over medium heat. Grease the skillet with a little butter or oil.
5. Pour about 1/4 cup of batter onto the skillet for each pancake. Use the back of a spoon or a ladle to spread the batter into a circle if needed.
6. Cook the pancakes for 2-3 minutes, or until bubbles form on the surface and the edges look set.
7. Flip the pancakes and cook for an additional 1-2 minutes, or until golden brown and cooked through.
8. Transfer the cooked pancakes to a plate and keep them warm while you cook the remaining batter, greasing the skillet as needed between batches.
9. Serve the buttermilk pancakes warm with maple syrup drizzled over the top.
10. Enjoy these fluffy, golden pancakes as a delicious breakfast or brunch treat!

Chocolate Eclair Cake

Ingredients:

For the filling:

- 2 (3.4 oz) packages instant vanilla pudding mix
- 3 cups cold milk
- 1 (8 oz) container whipped topping (such as Cool Whip), thawed

For the cake:

- 1 (16 oz) package graham crackers
- 2 cups milk chocolate chips
- 1/3 cup unsalted butter
- 1 cup granulated sugar
- 1/2 cup whole milk
- 1 teaspoon vanilla extract

Instructions:

1. In a large mixing bowl, whisk together the instant vanilla pudding mix and cold milk until smooth. Let it sit for about 5 minutes to thicken.
2. Fold the whipped topping into the pudding mixture until well combined. Refrigerate the filling while preparing the rest of the cake.
3. Line the bottom of a 9x13-inch baking dish with a layer of graham crackers, breaking them if needed to fit.
4. In a medium saucepan, combine the milk chocolate chips, unsalted butter, granulated sugar, and whole milk. Cook over medium heat, stirring constantly, until the chocolate chips are melted and the mixture is smooth. Remove from heat and stir in the vanilla extract.
5. Pour half of the chocolate mixture over the layer of graham crackers in the baking dish. Smooth it out evenly with a spatula.
6. Place another layer of graham crackers on top of the chocolate layer.
7. Pour the remaining chocolate mixture over the second layer of graham crackers. Smooth it out evenly.
8. Add the prepared pudding filling on top of the second chocolate layer, spreading it out evenly.
9. Add a final layer of graham crackers on top of the pudding filling.

10. Cover the baking dish with plastic wrap and refrigerate the chocolate eclair cake for at least 4 hours, or overnight, to allow the layers to set.
11. Once chilled, slice and serve the chocolate eclair cake cold. Enjoy this delicious and easy-to-make dessert!

Peanut Butter Fudge

Ingredients:

- 1 cup of creamy peanut butter
- 1 cup of unsalted butter
- 1 teaspoon of vanilla extract
- 4 cups of powdered sugar

Instructions:

1. Line an 8x8 inch baking dish with parchment paper or lightly grease it with butter.
2. In a medium-sized saucepan, melt the butter and peanut butter over low heat, stirring constantly until smooth and well combined.
3. Remove the saucepan from heat and stir in the vanilla extract.
4. Gradually add the powdered sugar, one cup at a time, stirring well after each addition until the mixture is smooth.
5. Pour the fudge mixture into the prepared baking dish and spread it evenly with a spatula.
6. Refrigerate the fudge for at least 2 hours, or until firm.
7. Once firm, remove the fudge from the baking dish and cut it into squares.
8. Serve and enjoy! Store any leftovers in an airtight container in the refrigerator.

Feel free to get creative with this recipe by adding chopped nuts, chocolate chips, or a swirl of chocolate on top for some extra indulgence!

Grandma's Snickerdoodle Bars

Ingredients:

- 2 1/3 cups all-purpose flour
- 1 teaspoon baking powder
- 1/2 teaspoon salt
- 1 cup unsalted butter, softened
- 1 1/4 cups granulated sugar
- 1/2 cup packed light brown sugar
- 3 large eggs
- 1 teaspoon vanilla extract
- 1 tablespoon ground cinnamon

For the cinnamon sugar topping:

- 2 tablespoons granulated sugar
- 1 tablespoon ground cinnamon

Instructions:

1. Preheat your oven to 350°F (175°C). Grease or line a 9x13-inch baking pan with parchment paper, leaving some overhang for easy removal.
2. In a medium bowl, whisk together the flour, baking powder, and salt. Set aside.
3. In a large mixing bowl, cream together the softened butter, granulated sugar, and brown sugar until light and fluffy, about 2-3 minutes.
4. Beat in the eggs, one at a time, until well combined. Stir in the vanilla extract.
5. Gradually add the dry ingredients to the wet ingredients, mixing until just combined. Be careful not to overmix.
6. Spread the dough evenly into the prepared baking pan, using a spatula to smooth the surface.
7. In a small bowl, mix together the 2 tablespoons of granulated sugar and 1 tablespoon of ground cinnamon for the topping. Sprinkle the cinnamon sugar mixture evenly over the dough in the pan.
8. Bake in the preheated oven for 25-30 minutes, or until the edges are golden brown and a toothpick inserted into the center comes out clean or with a few moist crumbs.
9. Allow the bars to cool completely in the pan on a wire rack before cutting into squares.
10. Serve and enjoy the delicious taste of Grandma's Snickerdoodle Bars!

These bars are perfect for sharing at gatherings or enjoying as a sweet treat with a cup of coffee or tea. They have all the flavors of traditional snickerdoodle cookies but in a convenient and portable form.

Black Forest Cake

Ingredients:

For the chocolate cake layers:

- 2 cups all-purpose flour
- 3/4 cup unsweetened cocoa powder
- 2 cups granulated sugar
- 2 teaspoons baking powder
- 1 1/2 teaspoons baking soda
- 1 teaspoon salt
- 2 large eggs
- 1 cup milk
- 1/2 cup vegetable oil
- 2 teaspoons vanilla extract
- 1 cup boiling water

For the cherry filling:

- 1 (21-ounce) can cherry pie filling

For the whipped cream frosting:

- 2 cups heavy cream, chilled
- 1/2 cup powdered sugar
- 1 teaspoon vanilla extract

For garnish:

- Chocolate shavings or curls
- Maraschino cherries

Instructions:

For the chocolate cake layers:

1. Preheat your oven to 350°F (175°C). Grease and flour two 9-inch round cake pans.
2. In a large mixing bowl, sift together the flour, cocoa powder, sugar, baking powder, baking soda, and salt.
3. Add the eggs, milk, oil, and vanilla extract to the dry ingredients. Beat on medium speed for 2 minutes.

4. Stir in the boiling water until the batter is well combined. The batter will be thin, but that's okay.
5. Pour the batter evenly into the prepared cake pans.
6. Bake in the preheated oven for 30 to 35 minutes, or until a toothpick inserted into the center comes out clean.
7. Allow the cakes to cool in the pans for 10 minutes, then transfer them to wire racks to cool completely.

For the whipped cream frosting:

1. In a large mixing bowl, beat the chilled heavy cream, powdered sugar, and vanilla extract together until stiff peaks form.

Assembling the cake:

1. Once the cake layers have cooled completely, place one layer on a serving plate or cake stand.
2. Spread half of the cherry pie filling evenly over the top of the first cake layer.
3. Spread a layer of whipped cream frosting over the cherry filling.
4. Place the second cake layer on top and repeat the process with the remaining cherry filling and whipped cream frosting.
5. Garnish the top of the cake with chocolate shavings or curls and maraschino cherries.
6. Refrigerate the cake for at least 1 hour before serving to allow the flavors to meld together.
7. Slice and serve the delicious Black Forest Cake!

This cake is a wonderful combination of moist chocolate cake, sweet cherry filling, and fluffy whipped cream frosting—a true crowd-pleaser for any occasion!

Lemon Poppy Seed Cake

Ingredients:

For the cake:

- 1 1/2 cups all-purpose flour
- 2 tablespoons poppy seeds
- 1 teaspoon baking powder
- 1/4 teaspoon baking soda
- 1/4 teaspoon salt
- 1/2 cup unsalted butter, softened
- 1 cup granulated sugar
- 2 large eggs
- 1 tablespoon lemon zest (from about 2 lemons)
- 1/4 cup fresh lemon juice
- 1/2 cup sour cream or Greek yogurt
- 1 teaspoon vanilla extract

For the lemon glaze:

- 1 cup powdered sugar
- 2-3 tablespoons fresh lemon juice

Optional garnish:

- Lemon zest
- Poppy seeds

Instructions:

For the cake:

1. Preheat your oven to 350°F (175°C). Grease and flour a 9x5-inch loaf pan.
2. In a medium bowl, whisk together the flour, poppy seeds, baking powder, baking soda, and salt. Set aside.
3. In a large mixing bowl, cream together the softened butter and granulated sugar until light and fluffy.
4. Beat in the eggs, one at a time, until well combined.
5. Mix in the lemon zest, lemon juice, sour cream (or Greek yogurt), and vanilla extract until smooth.
6. Gradually add the dry ingredients to the wet ingredients, mixing until just combined. Be careful not to overmix.

7. Pour the batter into the prepared loaf pan and smooth the top with a spatula.
8. Bake in the preheated oven for 45 to 55 minutes, or until a toothpick inserted into the center comes out clean.
9. Remove the cake from the oven and allow it to cool in the pan for about 10 minutes. Then, transfer it to a wire rack to cool completely.

For the lemon glaze:

1. In a small bowl, whisk together the powdered sugar and fresh lemon juice until smooth. Adjust the consistency by adding more lemon juice if needed.
2. Once the cake has cooled, drizzle the lemon glaze over the top of the cake.
3. Optionally, garnish the cake with additional lemon zest and poppy seeds for decoration.
4. Allow the glaze to set before slicing and serving.

This Lemon Poppy Seed Cake is perfect for any occasion, whether you're serving it as a dessert, snack, or even for breakfast or brunch! Its bright lemon flavor and tender crumb make it a favorite among lemon lovers.

Classic Tiramisu

Ingredients:

- 6 large egg yolks
- 3/4 cup granulated sugar
- 1 cup mascarpone cheese, softened
- 1 1/2 cups heavy cream
- 1 1/2 cups strong brewed coffee, cooled to room temperature
- 2 tablespoons coffee liqueur (optional)
- 1 teaspoon vanilla extract
- 2 (7-ounce) packages of ladyfinger cookies (savoiardi)
- Unsweetened cocoa powder, for dusting

Instructions:

1. In a heatproof bowl, whisk together the egg yolks and granulated sugar until well combined.
2. Place the bowl over a pot of simmering water (double boiler), making sure the bottom of the bowl does not touch the water. Cook the egg yolk mixture, whisking constantly, until thickened and pale yellow in color, about 5-7 minutes.
3. Remove the bowl from the heat and let it cool slightly. Then, whisk in the mascarpone cheese until smooth and well combined. Set aside.
4. In a separate mixing bowl, whip the heavy cream until stiff peaks form.
5. Gently fold the whipped cream into the mascarpone mixture until no streaks remain. Be careful not to overmix.
6. In a shallow dish, combine the cooled brewed coffee and coffee liqueur (if using).
7. Dip each ladyfinger cookie into the coffee mixture, soaking them for just a few seconds on each side. Do not oversoak, as the cookies can become too soggy.
8. Arrange a layer of soaked ladyfinger cookies in the bottom of a 9x13-inch baking dish, breaking them if necessary to fit.
9. Spread half of the mascarpone mixture evenly over the layer of ladyfingers.
10. Repeat the layers, starting with another layer of soaked ladyfinger cookies and finishing with the remaining mascarpone mixture on top.
11. Cover the tiramisu with plastic wrap and refrigerate for at least 4 hours, or preferably overnight, to allow the flavors to meld together and the dessert to set.
12. Before serving, dust the top of the tiramisu with unsweetened cocoa powder using a fine-mesh sieve.
13. Slice and serve the classic tiramisu chilled, and enjoy the creamy, coffee-infused layers!

This classic tiramisu recipe is perfect for special occasions or whenever you're craving a decadent and elegant dessert with a delightful balance of flavors.

Chocolate Covered Strawberries

Ingredients:

- Fresh strawberries, washed and dried thoroughly
- Semi-sweet, dark, or white chocolate (chips, bars, or melting wafers)
- Optional: White chocolate for drizzling, chopped nuts, shredded coconut, or sprinkles for decorating

Instructions:

1. Prepare the Strawberries:
    - Make sure the strawberries are completely dry before dipping to prevent the chocolate from seizing.
    - Line a baking sheet with parchment paper or wax paper to place the dipped strawberries on.
2. Melt the Chocolate:
    - Chop the chocolate into small, uniform pieces for even melting.
    - Place the chocolate in a microwave-safe bowl or a heatproof bowl set over a pot of simmering water (double boiler method).
    - Microwave in 30-second intervals, stirring between each interval, until the chocolate is melted and smooth. Be careful not to overheat the chocolate.
3. Dip the Strawberries:
    - Hold each strawberry by the stem and dip it into the melted chocolate, swirling to coat it evenly.
    - Allow any excess chocolate to drip back into the bowl.
    - Place the dipped strawberry on the prepared baking sheet.
4. Decorate (Optional):
    - If desired, sprinkle chopped nuts, shredded coconut, or sprinkles over the chocolate before it sets.
    - For an extra touch, melt some white chocolate and drizzle it over the dipped strawberries using a fork or piping bag.
5. Set and Chill:
    - Once all the strawberries are dipped and decorated, place the baking sheet in the refrigerator for about 30 minutes to allow the chocolate to set completely.
6. Serve and Enjoy:
    - Once the chocolate has hardened, transfer the chocolate covered strawberries to a serving plate or platter.
    - Enjoy them immediately, or store any leftovers in the refrigerator for up to 2 days.

Chocolate covered strawberries are perfect for special occasions like Valentine's Day, anniversaries, or as a sweet indulgence any time of the year. They're simple to make but look and taste incredibly impressive!

Grandma's Bread and Butter Pudding

Ingredients:

- 8 slices of bread (white or whole wheat), crusts removed
- Butter, softened
- 3/4 cup raisins or sultanas
- 4 large eggs
- 2 cups whole milk
- 1/2 cup heavy cream (optional, for extra richness)
- 1/2 cup granulated sugar
- 1 teaspoon vanilla extract
- 1/2 teaspoon ground cinnamon
- Pinch of nutmeg
- Pinch of salt

Instructions:

1. Preheat your oven to 350°F (175°C). Grease a baking dish with butter.
2. Butter each slice of bread generously on one side. Cut the slices diagonally into triangles.
3. Arrange half of the buttered bread triangles in the prepared baking dish, overlapping them slightly. Sprinkle half of the raisins over the bread.
4. Arrange the remaining bread triangles over the first layer and sprinkle the rest of the raisins on top.
5. In a mixing bowl, whisk together the eggs, milk, heavy cream (if using), sugar, vanilla extract, cinnamon, nutmeg, and salt until well combined.
6. Pour the egg mixture evenly over the bread slices, ensuring that all the bread is soaked.
7. Let the bread soak in the egg mixture for about 15-20 minutes, pressing down gently with a fork or spatula to ensure the bread absorbs the liquid.
8. Place the baking dish in the preheated oven and bake for 40-45 minutes, or until the pudding is set and the top is golden brown.
9. Remove the bread and butter pudding from the oven and let it cool slightly before serving.
10. Serve warm, optionally with a dusting of powdered sugar or a dollop of whipped cream or vanilla ice cream.

Grandma's Bread and Butter Pudding is a timeless dessert that's perfect for cozy evenings or special occasions. The combination of soft, custardy bread with plump raisins and warm spices is simply irresistible!

Old-Fashioned Sugar Cookies

Ingredients:

- 2 3/4 cups all-purpose flour
- 1 teaspoon baking soda
- 1/2 teaspoon baking powder
- 1 cup unsalted butter, softened
- 1 1/2 cups granulated sugar
- 1 large egg
- 2 teaspoons vanilla extract
- Additional sugar for rolling (optional)
- Sprinkles or colored sugar for decorating (optional)

Instructions:

1. Preheat your oven to 375°F (190°C). Line baking sheets with parchment paper or silicone baking mats.
2. In a medium bowl, whisk together the flour, baking soda, and baking powder. Set aside.
3. In a large mixing bowl, cream together the softened butter and granulated sugar until light and fluffy, about 2-3 minutes.
4. Beat in the egg and vanilla extract until well combined.
5. Gradually add the dry ingredients to the wet ingredients, mixing until a dough forms. If the dough is too soft, you can refrigerate it for about 30 minutes to make it easier to handle.
6. If desired, you can roll portions of the dough into balls and then roll them in additional sugar for a sparkly finish.
7. Place the cookie dough balls onto the prepared baking sheets, spacing them about 2 inches apart. Flatten each cookie slightly with the palm of your hand.
8. If using, decorate the cookies with sprinkles or colored sugar.
9. Bake in the preheated oven for 8-10 minutes, or until the edges are lightly golden brown.
10. Allow the cookies to cool on the baking sheets for a few minutes before transferring them to wire racks to cool completely.
11. Once cooled, store the cookies in an airtight container at room temperature for up to one week.

These old-fashioned sugar cookies are perfect for any occasion, from holiday celebrations to everyday snacking. They have a wonderfully buttery flavor and a soft, tender texture that's sure to please everyone!

Peach Melba

Ingredients:

- 4 ripe peaches
- 1/2 cup granulated sugar
- 1/2 cup water
- 1 teaspoon lemon juice
- 1 cup fresh raspberries
- Vanilla ice cream
- Fresh mint leaves, for garnish (optional)

Instructions:

1. Prepare the Peaches:
    - Bring a pot of water to a boil. Using a sharp knife, score a small "X" on the bottom of each peach.
    - Carefully place the peaches in the boiling water for about 30 seconds, then transfer them to a bowl of ice water to cool.
    - Once cooled, peel the skin off the peaches. Cut the peaches in half and remove the pits. Slice each peach half into wedges or chunks.
2. Make the Raspberry Sauce:
    - In a small saucepan, combine the raspberries, granulated sugar, water, and lemon juice.
    - Bring the mixture to a simmer over medium heat, stirring occasionally.
    - Cook for about 5-7 minutes, or until the raspberries have broken down and the sauce has thickened slightly.
    - Remove the saucepan from the heat and strain the raspberry mixture through a fine-mesh sieve to remove the seeds. Allow the sauce to cool.
3. Assemble the Peach Melba:
    - Divide the sliced peaches among serving bowls or plates.
    - Top the peaches with a scoop of vanilla ice cream.
    - Drizzle the raspberry sauce over the ice cream and peaches.
4. Garnish and Serve:
    - Garnish the Peach Melba with fresh mint leaves, if desired.
    - Serve immediately and enjoy!

Peach Melba is a lovely dessert that's perfect for showcasing the sweetness of ripe peaches and the tartness of fresh raspberries. The combination of flavors and textures, along with the creamy vanilla ice cream, makes it a delightful treat for any occasion.

Chocolate Cream Pie

Ingredients:

For the pie crust:

- 1 1/4 cups all-purpose flour
- 1/2 teaspoon salt
- 1/2 cup (1 stick) unsalted butter, chilled and cut into small pieces
- 3-4 tablespoons ice water

For the chocolate filling:

- 1/2 cup granulated sugar
- 1/4 cup cornstarch
- 1/4 teaspoon salt
- 2 1/2 cups whole milk
- 4 large egg yolks
- 6 ounces semi-sweet chocolate, chopped
- 1 teaspoon vanilla extract

For the whipped cream topping:

- 1 cup heavy cream
- 2 tablespoons powdered sugar
- 1/2 teaspoon vanilla extract

Instructions:

For the pie crust:

1. In a large mixing bowl, whisk together the flour and salt.
2. Add the chilled butter pieces to the flour mixture. Use a pastry cutter or your fingertips to cut the butter into the flour until the mixture resembles coarse crumbs.
3. Gradually add the ice water, 1 tablespoon at a time, mixing with a fork until the dough comes together.
4. Shape the dough into a disk, wrap it in plastic wrap, and refrigerate for at least 30 minutes.
5. Preheat your oven to 375°F (190°C). Roll out the chilled dough on a lightly floured surface into a circle large enough to fit a 9-inch pie dish.
6. Transfer the rolled-out dough to the pie dish, pressing it gently into the bottom and sides. Trim any excess dough and crimp the edges. Prick the bottom of the crust with a fork.

7. Line the crust with parchment paper or aluminum foil and fill it with pie weights or dried beans.
8. Bake the crust in the preheated oven for 15 minutes. Remove the weights and parchment paper/foil, then bake for an additional 10-12 minutes, or until the crust is golden brown. Allow the crust to cool completely.

For the chocolate filling:

1. In a medium saucepan, whisk together the granulated sugar, cornstarch, and salt.
2. Gradually whisk in the whole milk until smooth.
3. Place the saucepan over medium heat and cook, stirring constantly, until the mixture thickens and comes to a boil.
4. Boil for 1-2 minutes, then remove the saucepan from the heat.
5. In a separate bowl, whisk the egg yolks. Gradually whisk in about 1/2 cup of the hot milk mixture to temper the eggs.
6. Gradually pour the tempered egg mixture back into the saucepan, whisking constantly.
7. Place the saucepan back over medium heat and cook, stirring constantly, until the mixture thickens further, about 2-3 minutes.
8. Remove the saucepan from the heat and stir in the chopped chocolate and vanilla extract until the chocolate is melted and the filling is smooth.
9. Pour the chocolate filling into the cooled pie crust, spreading it evenly. Place a piece of plastic wrap directly on the surface of the filling to prevent a skin from forming. Refrigerate the pie until the filling is set, at least 4 hours or overnight.

For the whipped cream topping:

1. In a mixing bowl, beat the heavy cream, powdered sugar, and vanilla extract together until stiff peaks form.
2. Spread or pipe the whipped cream over the chilled chocolate filling.

Serve:

1. Slice and serve the chocolate cream pie chilled, and enjoy!

This chocolate cream pie is sure to satisfy any chocolate lover's cravings with its creamy, indulgent filling and light, fluffy whipped cream topping.

Grandma's Pumpkin Bread

Ingredients:

- 1 3/4 cups all-purpose flour
- 1 teaspoon baking soda
- 1/2 teaspoon baking powder
- 1 teaspoon ground cinnamon
- 1/2 teaspoon ground nutmeg
- 1/2 teaspoon ground ginger
- 1/4 teaspoon ground cloves
- 1/2 teaspoon salt
- 1/2 cup unsalted butter, melted and cooled
- 1 cup granulated sugar
- 1/2 cup packed light brown sugar
- 2 large eggs
- 1 teaspoon vanilla extract
- 1 cup canned pumpkin puree (not pumpkin pie filling)
- 1/3 cup milk
- Optional: 1/2 cup chopped nuts (such as pecans or walnuts)

Instructions:

1. Preheat your oven to 350°F (175°C). Grease and flour a 9x5-inch loaf pan, or line it with parchment paper for easy removal.
2. In a medium bowl, whisk together the flour, baking soda, baking powder, cinnamon, nutmeg, ginger, cloves, and salt. Set aside.
3. In a large mixing bowl, whisk together the melted butter, granulated sugar, and brown sugar until well combined.
4. Add the eggs, one at a time, beating well after each addition. Stir in the vanilla extract.
5. Add the pumpkin puree to the wet ingredients and mix until smooth.
6. Gradually add the dry ingredients to the wet ingredients, alternating with the milk, and mix until just combined. Be careful not to overmix. If using nuts, fold them into the batter.
7. Pour the batter into the prepared loaf pan and spread it evenly.
8. Bake in the preheated oven for 55-65 minutes, or until a toothpick inserted into the center comes out clean. If the top of the bread is browning too quickly, you can tent it with aluminum foil halfway through baking.

9. Allow the pumpkin bread to cool in the pan for 10 minutes, then transfer it to a wire rack to cool completely before slicing.
10. Slice and serve the pumpkin bread, and enjoy the cozy flavors of fall!

This pumpkin bread is perfect for breakfast, brunch, or as a snack any time of day. It's wonderfully moist and flavorful, with just the right amount of spice. Plus, it's a great way to use up any leftover canned pumpkin you might have on hand.

Classic Cheesecake

Ingredients:

For the crust:

- 1 1/2 cups graham cracker crumbs (about 12 whole graham crackers)
- 1/4 cup granulated sugar
- 6 tablespoons unsalted butter, melted

For the cheesecake filling:

- 4 (8-ounce) packages cream cheese, softened
- 1 1/4 cups granulated sugar
- 4 large eggs
- 2 teaspoons vanilla extract
- 1 cup sour cream

Instructions:

For the crust:

1. Preheat your oven to 325°F (160°C). Grease a 9-inch springform pan with butter or cooking spray.
2. In a medium bowl, mix together the graham cracker crumbs, granulated sugar, and melted butter until well combined and the mixture resembles wet sand.
3. Press the crumb mixture firmly and evenly into the bottom of the prepared springform pan, using the bottom of a flat glass or measuring cup to help compact the crumbs.
4. Bake the crust in the preheated oven for 10 minutes. Remove from the oven and let it cool while you prepare the cheesecake filling.

For the cheesecake filling:

1. In a large mixing bowl, beat the softened cream cheese and granulated sugar together with an electric mixer on medium speed until smooth and creamy, about 2-3 minutes.
2. Add the eggs one at a time, beating well after each addition. Scrape down the sides of the bowl as needed.

3. Mix in the vanilla extract until well combined.
4. Add the sour cream and beat on low speed until incorporated.
5. Pour the cheesecake filling over the cooled crust in the springform pan.
6. Tap the pan gently on the counter to release any air bubbles.
7. Place the springform pan on a baking sheet to catch any drips, then bake in the preheated oven for 55-60 minutes, or until the edges of the cheesecake are set but the center is still slightly jiggly.
8. Turn off the oven and leave the cheesecake inside with the door closed for 1 hour to cool gradually.
9. After 1 hour, remove the cheesecake from the oven and run a knife around the edge of the pan to loosen the cheesecake from the sides. This will help prevent cracking as it cools.
10. Allow the cheesecake to cool completely at room temperature, then refrigerate for at least 4 hours or overnight to chill and set completely.
11. Once chilled, remove the sides of the springform pan. Slice and serve the classic cheesecake plain or with your favorite toppings, such as fresh berries, fruit compote, or whipped cream.
12. Enjoy the creamy, decadent goodness of classic cheesecake!

This classic cheesecake recipe is perfect for any occasion and is sure to impress your friends and family with its rich flavor and creamy texture.

www.ingramcontent.com/pod-product-compliance
Lightning Source LLC
LaVergne TN
LVHW081613060526
838201LV00054B/2227